50 Busy Family Dinner Meal Ideas

By: Kelly Johnson

Table of Contents

- One-Pot Spaghetti Bolognese
- Sheet Pan Chicken and Vegetables
- Beef and Broccoli Stir-Fry
- Slow Cooker Chili
- Baked Ziti with Spinach
- BBQ Chicken Flatbread
- Veggie-Packed Fried Rice
- Turkey Taco Bowls
- Creamy Garlic Shrimp Pasta
- Cheeseburger Casserole
- Lemon Herb Grilled Salmon
- Chicken Alfredo Bake
- Vegetable Stir-Fry with Rice
- Loaded Baked Potatoes
- Quick Chicken Quesadillas
- Pulled Pork Sliders
- Margherita Flatbread Pizza
- Sausage and Peppers over Rice
- Sweet and Sour Chicken
- One-Pan Lemon Garlic Chicken
- Meatball Subs
- Teriyaki Beef Bowls
- Buffalo Chicken Wraps
- Vegetarian Stuffed Peppers
- Grilled Cheese and Tomato Soup
- BBQ Ribs with Cornbread
- Turkey and Cheese Roll-Ups
- Chicken and Rice Casserole
- Beef Tacos with Guacamole
- Roasted Veggie Pasta Bake
- Sloppy Joes with Coleslaw
- Tuna Casserole
- Black Bean Enchiladas
- Baked Mac and Cheese
- Grilled Chicken Caesar Wraps

- Ham and Cheese Stromboli
- Pesto Pasta with Cherry Tomatoes
- Shrimp Tacos with Mango Salsa
- Veggie and Cheese Quiche
- Chicken Parmesan Sandwiches
- Steak and Potato Skillet
- Lentil Soup with Crusty Bread
- BBQ Meatball Subs
- Teriyaki Tofu Stir-Fry
- Veggie Burgers with Sweet Potato Fries
- Mini Personal Pizzas
- Chicken Fajitas with Tortillas
- Quick Shepherd's Pie
- Spinach and Mushroom Lasagna
- Pork Chops with Mashed Potatoes

One-Pot Spaghetti Bolognese

Ingredients:

- 1 lb ground beef
- 1 small onion, diced
- 2 cloves garlic, minced
- 1 can (14 oz) diced tomatoes
- 2 cups marinara sauce
- 3 cups chicken or beef broth
- 12 oz spaghetti
- 1 teaspoon Italian seasoning
- Salt and pepper, to taste
- Grated Parmesan and fresh basil for garnish

Instructions:

1. In a large pot, cook ground beef over medium heat until browned. Drain excess fat.
2. Add onion and garlic, cooking until softened.
3. Stir in diced tomatoes, marinara sauce, broth, Italian seasoning, salt, and pepper.
4. Break the spaghetti in half and stir into the pot. Ensure the liquid covers the pasta.
5. Bring to a boil, then reduce heat and simmer, stirring occasionally, until the pasta is cooked (about 10-12 minutes).
6. Garnish with Parmesan and basil before serving.

Sheet Pan Chicken and Vegetables

Ingredients:

- 4 chicken thighs or breasts
- 2 cups broccoli florets
- 1 red bell pepper, sliced
- 1 zucchini, sliced
- 2 tablespoons olive oil
- 1 teaspoon garlic powder
- 1 teaspoon paprika
- 1/2 teaspoon dried thyme
- Salt and pepper, to taste

Instructions:

1. Preheat oven to 425°F (220°C) and line a baking sheet with parchment paper.
2. Arrange chicken and vegetables on the sheet pan.
3. Drizzle olive oil over everything, then sprinkle with garlic powder, paprika, thyme, salt, and pepper. Toss to coat evenly.
4. Bake for 25-30 minutes, flipping halfway through, until chicken is cooked and vegetables are tender.

Beef and Broccoli Stir-Fry

Ingredients:

- 1 lb flank steak, thinly sliced
- 2 cups broccoli florets
- 1/4 cup soy sauce
- 2 tablespoons oyster sauce
- 1 tablespoon sesame oil
- 1 teaspoon cornstarch
- 2 tablespoons vegetable oil
- 1 clove garlic, minced
- Cooked rice, for serving

Instructions:

1. Whisk soy sauce, oyster sauce, sesame oil, and cornstarch in a bowl. Add steak and marinate for 15 minutes.
2. Heat vegetable oil in a skillet or wok. Stir-fry broccoli for 3-4 minutes, then set aside.
3. Add steak and garlic to the skillet, cooking until browned.
4. Return broccoli to the pan, tossing everything in the sauce until heated through. Serve over rice.

Slow Cooker Chili

Ingredients:

- 1 lb ground beef or turkey
- 1 small onion, diced
- 2 cans (15 oz each) kidney beans, drained
- 1 can (14 oz) diced tomatoes
- 1 cup tomato sauce
- 1 tablespoon chili powder
- 1 teaspoon cumin
- 1 teaspoon smoked paprika
- Salt and pepper, to taste
- Optional toppings: shredded cheese, sour cream, green onions

Instructions:

1. Brown ground beef and onion in a skillet, then transfer to a slow cooker.
2. Add beans, tomatoes, tomato sauce, and spices. Stir to combine.
3. Cook on low for 6-8 hours or high for 3-4 hours.
4. Serve with desired toppings.

Baked Ziti with Spinach

Ingredients:

- 12 oz ziti pasta
- 2 cups marinara sauce
- 1 cup ricotta cheese
- 2 cups fresh spinach, chopped
- 1 cup shredded mozzarella
- 1/2 cup grated Parmesan

Instructions:

1. Preheat oven to 375°F (190°C). Cook pasta according to package instructions. Drain.
2. Mix marinara sauce, ricotta, spinach, and half the mozzarella in a large bowl. Add pasta and toss to coat.
3. Transfer to a greased baking dish. Top with remaining mozzarella and Parmesan.
4. Bake for 20-25 minutes, until bubbly and golden.

BBQ Chicken Flatbread

Ingredients:

- 2 flatbreads or naan
- 1/2 cup barbecue sauce
- 1 cup cooked shredded chicken
- 1/2 cup shredded mozzarella
- 1/4 cup red onion, thinly sliced
- Optional toppings: fresh cilantro

Instructions:

1. Preheat oven to 400°F (200°C). Place flatbreads on a baking sheet.
2. Spread barbecue sauce over each flatbread. Top with chicken, cheese, and onion.
3. Bake for 10-12 minutes, until the cheese is melted. Garnish with cilantro if desired.

Veggie-Packed Fried Rice

Ingredients:

- 2 cups cooked rice, chilled
- 1 tablespoon vegetable oil
- 1 cup mixed vegetables (carrots, peas, bell peppers)
- 2 eggs, beaten
- 2 tablespoons soy sauce
- 1 tablespoon sesame oil
- 2 green onions, sliced

Instructions:

1. Heat vegetable oil in a large skillet or wok. Sauté vegetables until tender.
2. Push veggies to one side and scramble the eggs in the empty space.
3. Add rice, soy sauce, and sesame oil, stirring to combine. Cook until heated through.
4. Sprinkle with green onions before serving.

Turkey Taco Bowls

Ingredients:

- 1 lb ground turkey
- 1 tablespoon taco seasoning
- 1 cup cooked rice or quinoa
- 1 cup black beans, drained
- 1/2 cup corn kernels
- 1 cup diced tomatoes
- Optional toppings: shredded lettuce, cheese, salsa, sour cream

Instructions:

1. Brown ground turkey in a skillet and season with taco seasoning.
2. Assemble bowls with rice or quinoa as the base. Add turkey, beans, corn, and tomatoes.
3. Top with desired toppings and serve.

Creamy Garlic Shrimp Pasta

Ingredients:

- 12 oz spaghetti or fettuccine
- 1 lb large shrimp, peeled and deveined
- 3 tablespoons butter
- 3 cloves garlic, minced
- 1 cup heavy cream
- 1/2 cup grated Parmesan
- Salt and pepper, to taste
- Fresh parsley for garnish

Instructions:

1. Cook pasta according to package instructions. Reserve 1/2 cup pasta water.
2. In a skillet, melt butter and sauté garlic until fragrant. Add shrimp and cook until pink.
3. Pour in cream and Parmesan, stirring until smooth. Add pasta water if the sauce is too thick.
4. Toss in cooked pasta and mix until coated. Garnish with parsley before serving.

Cheeseburger Casserole

Ingredients:

- 1 lb ground beef
- 1 small onion, diced
- 2 cloves garlic, minced
- 1 can (14 oz) diced tomatoes
- 1/4 cup ketchup
- 2 cups cooked macaroni
- 1 1/2 cups shredded cheddar cheese
- Salt and pepper, to taste

Instructions:

1. Preheat oven to 375°F (190°C).
2. Brown ground beef with onion and garlic in a skillet. Drain excess fat.
3. Stir in diced tomatoes, ketchup, salt, and pepper. Simmer for 5 minutes.
4. Mix cooked macaroni with the beef mixture and half the cheese. Transfer to a baking dish.
5. Sprinkle remaining cheese on top. Bake for 15-20 minutes until bubbly and golden.

Lemon Herb Grilled Salmon

Ingredients:

- 4 salmon fillets
- 2 tablespoons olive oil
- Juice of 1 lemon
- 2 cloves garlic, minced
- 1 teaspoon dried oregano
- 1 teaspoon dried thyme
- Salt and pepper, to taste

Instructions:

1. In a bowl, whisk together olive oil, lemon juice, garlic, oregano, thyme, salt, and pepper.
2. Marinate salmon fillets in the mixture for 15-20 minutes.
3. Preheat grill or grill pan to medium heat.
4. Grill salmon for 4-5 minutes per side, or until cooked through. Serve immediately.

Chicken Alfredo Bake

Ingredients:

- 12 oz pasta (penne or fettuccine)
- 2 cups cooked shredded chicken
- 2 cups Alfredo sauce
- 1 cup shredded mozzarella cheese
- 1/2 cup grated Parmesan
- Optional: fresh parsley for garnish

Instructions:

1. Preheat oven to 375°F (190°C). Cook pasta according to package instructions. Drain.
2. Mix cooked pasta, chicken, and Alfredo sauce in a large bowl. Transfer to a greased baking dish.
3. Sprinkle mozzarella and Parmesan on top.
4. Bake for 20-25 minutes, until bubbly and golden. Garnish with parsley before serving.

Vegetable Stir-Fry with Rice

Ingredients:

- 2 cups mixed vegetables (broccoli, bell peppers, carrots, snap peas)
- 2 tablespoons vegetable oil
- 2 tablespoons soy sauce
- 1 tablespoon oyster sauce
- 1 teaspoon sesame oil
- 1 teaspoon cornstarch mixed with 2 tablespoons water
- Cooked rice, for serving

Instructions:

1. Heat vegetable oil in a wok or skillet. Sauté vegetables until tender but crisp.
2. Mix soy sauce, oyster sauce, and sesame oil in a bowl. Add to the pan and stir.
3. Stir in cornstarch mixture to thicken the sauce. Cook for 1-2 minutes.
4. Serve stir-fry over cooked rice.

Loaded Baked Potatoes

Ingredients:

- 4 large baking potatoes
- 1 cup shredded cheddar cheese
- 1/2 cup cooked bacon bits
- 1/2 cup sour cream
- 2 green onions, sliced
- Salt and pepper, to taste

Instructions:

1. Preheat oven to 400°F (200°C). Bake potatoes for 1 hour, or until tender.
2. Slice open each potato and fluff the insides with a fork. Season with salt and pepper.
3. Top with cheese, bacon, sour cream, and green onions. Serve hot.

Quick Chicken Quesadillas

Ingredients:

- 2 cups cooked shredded chicken
- 1 cup shredded Mexican cheese blend
- 4 large tortillas
- 2 tablespoons vegetable oil
- Optional: salsa, sour cream, guacamole for serving

Instructions:

1. Heat a large skillet over medium heat. Place one tortilla in the skillet.
2. Sprinkle chicken and cheese evenly over half the tortilla. Fold the other half over.
3. Cook for 2-3 minutes per side, until golden and cheese is melted. Repeat with remaining tortillas.
4. Slice into wedges and serve with salsa, sour cream, or guacamole.

Pulled Pork Sliders

Ingredients:

- 2 cups cooked pulled pork
- 1/2 cup barbecue sauce
- 8 slider buns
- Optional: coleslaw for topping

Instructions:

1. Heat pulled pork in a skillet and mix with barbecue sauce.
2. Toast slider buns lightly.
3. Assemble sliders with pulled pork and optional coleslaw. Serve warm.

Margherita Flatbread Pizza

Ingredients:

- 2 flatbreads or naan
- 1/2 cup marinara sauce
- 1 cup fresh mozzarella slices
- 1/4 cup fresh basil leaves
- 1 tablespoon olive oil

Instructions:

1. Preheat oven to 400°F (200°C). Place flatbreads on a baking sheet.
2. Spread marinara sauce over each flatbread. Top with mozzarella slices.
3. Bake for 8-10 minutes, until cheese is melted.
4. Garnish with fresh basil and drizzle with olive oil before serving.

Sausage and Peppers over Rice

Ingredients:

- 1 lb Italian sausage, sliced
- 1 red bell pepper, sliced
- 1 green bell pepper, sliced
- 1 small onion, sliced
- 2 cups cooked rice
- 1 tablespoon olive oil

Instructions:

1. Heat olive oil in a skillet. Cook sausage until browned.
2. Add bell peppers and onion, sautéing until tender.
3. Serve sausage and peppers over cooked rice.

Sweet and Sour Chicken

Ingredients:

- 1 lb chicken breast, cubed
- 1/4 cup cornstarch
- 2 tablespoons vegetable oil
- 1/2 cup pineapple chunks
- 1/2 red bell pepper, diced
- 1/2 cup sweet and sour sauce

Instructions:

1. Coat chicken pieces in cornstarch. Heat oil in a skillet and cook chicken until golden.
2. Add pineapple and bell pepper, stirring for 2-3 minutes.
3. Pour in sweet and sour sauce, tossing to coat. Cook until heated through. Serve hot.

One-Pan Lemon Garlic Chicken

Ingredients:

- 4 chicken thighs or breasts
- 2 tablespoons olive oil
- 3 cloves garlic, minced
- Juice of 1 lemon
- 1 teaspoon dried thyme
- 1 teaspoon paprika
- Salt and pepper, to taste
- 1 cup green beans or asparagus

Instructions:

1. Preheat oven to 375°F (190°C). Heat olive oil in an oven-safe skillet over medium heat.
2. Season chicken with thyme, paprika, salt, and pepper. Sear both sides until golden, about 3 minutes per side.
3. Add garlic to the skillet, followed by lemon juice. Arrange green beans or asparagus around the chicken.
4. Transfer skillet to oven and bake for 15-20 minutes, until chicken is cooked through.

Meatball Subs

Ingredients:

- 12-16 cooked meatballs
- 2 cups marinara sauce
- 4 hoagie rolls
- 1 cup shredded mozzarella cheese
- Optional: grated Parmesan for topping

Instructions:

1. Heat meatballs in marinara sauce on the stovetop.
2. Toast hoagie rolls lightly in the oven or on a skillet.
3. Fill rolls with meatballs and sauce, then sprinkle with mozzarella.
4. Place subs under the broiler for 1-2 minutes, until cheese is melted.

Teriyaki Beef Bowls

Ingredients:

- 1 lb ground beef
- 1/4 cup teriyaki sauce
- 2 cups cooked rice
- 1 cup steamed broccoli
- 1 tablespoon sesame seeds for garnish

Instructions:

1. Brown ground beef in a skillet. Drain excess fat.
2. Stir in teriyaki sauce and simmer for 2 minutes.
3. Serve beef over rice, topped with steamed broccoli and sesame seeds.

Buffalo Chicken Wraps

Ingredients:

- 2 cups cooked shredded chicken
- 1/4 cup buffalo sauce
- 4 tortillas
- 1 cup shredded lettuce
- 1/2 cup diced tomatoes
- 1/4 cup ranch or blue cheese dressing

Instructions:

1. Toss shredded chicken with buffalo sauce in a bowl.
2. Fill tortillas with chicken, lettuce, tomatoes, and dressing.
3. Wrap tightly and serve immediately.

Vegetarian Stuffed Peppers

Ingredients:

- 4 large bell peppers, halved and seeded
- 1 cup cooked quinoa or rice
- 1 cup black beans
- 1/2 cup corn
- 1 cup shredded cheese
- 1/2 cup salsa

Instructions:

1. Preheat oven to 375°F (190°C). Place bell pepper halves in a baking dish.
2. Mix quinoa, black beans, corn, half the cheese, and salsa in a bowl.
3. Stuff mixture into bell peppers. Sprinkle remaining cheese on top.
4. Bake for 25-30 minutes, until peppers are tender.

Grilled Cheese and Tomato Soup

Ingredients for Grilled Cheese:

- 4 slices of bread
- 4 slices of cheese (cheddar, Swiss, or American)
- 2 tablespoons butter

Ingredients for Tomato Soup:

- 1 can (14 oz) crushed tomatoes
- 1 cup chicken or vegetable broth
- 1/2 cup heavy cream
- Salt and pepper, to taste

Instructions:

1. For grilled cheese, butter one side of each bread slice. Sandwich cheese between unbuttered sides. Cook in a skillet until golden and melted.
2. For soup, heat crushed tomatoes and broth in a saucepan. Simmer for 10 minutes. Stir in cream, salt, and pepper.
3. Serve soup alongside grilled cheese.

BBQ Ribs with Cornbread

Ingredients for Ribs:

- 2 racks pork ribs
- 1 cup BBQ sauce
- Salt and pepper

Ingredients for Cornbread:

- 1 cup cornmeal
- 1 cup all-purpose flour
- 1/4 cup sugar
- 1 tablespoon baking powder
- 1 cup milk
- 1 egg
- 1/4 cup melted butter

Instructions:

1. Preheat oven to 300°F (150°C). Season ribs with salt and pepper. Wrap in foil and bake for 2.5 hours.
2. Brush ribs with BBQ sauce and broil for 5-10 minutes until caramelized.
3. For cornbread, mix dry ingredients in one bowl and wet ingredients in another. Combine and pour into a greased pan. Bake at 375°F (190°C) for 20-25 minutes.

Turkey and Cheese Roll-Ups

Ingredients:

- 4 large tortillas
- 8 slices turkey
- 4 slices cheese (cheddar, Swiss, or provolone)
- 1/4 cup mayonnaise or cream cheese
- Optional: lettuce and tomato slices

Instructions:

1. Spread mayonnaise or cream cheese over each tortilla.
2. Layer turkey, cheese, and optional lettuce and tomato.
3. Roll up tightly, slice into pinwheels if desired, and serve.

Chicken and Rice Casserole

Ingredients:

- 2 cups cooked shredded chicken
- 2 cups cooked rice
- 1 can (10 oz) cream of chicken soup
- 1 cup shredded cheddar cheese
- 1/2 cup frozen peas or mixed vegetables

Instructions:

1. Preheat oven to 375°F (190°C).
2. Mix chicken, rice, soup, vegetables, and half the cheese in a bowl. Transfer to a greased baking dish.
3. Sprinkle remaining cheese on top. Bake for 20-25 minutes, until bubbly.

Beef Tacos with Guacamole

Ingredients:

- 1 lb ground beef
- 1 packet taco seasoning
- 8 taco shells
- 1 cup shredded lettuce
- 1/2 cup diced tomatoes
- 1/2 cup guacamole

Instructions:

1. Brown ground beef in a skillet. Stir in taco seasoning and cook according to package directions.
2. Fill taco shells with beef, lettuce, tomatoes, and guacamole. Serve immediately.

Roasted Veggie Pasta Bake

Ingredients:

- 3 cups mixed roasted vegetables (zucchini, bell peppers, cherry tomatoes)
- 12 oz cooked pasta (penne or rigatoni)
- 1 cup marinara sauce
- 1 cup shredded mozzarella cheese
- 1/2 cup grated Parmesan

Instructions:

1. Preheat oven to 375°F (190°C).
2. Mix roasted vegetables, pasta, and marinara sauce in a bowl. Transfer to a baking dish.
3. Top with mozzarella and Parmesan. Bake for 15-20 minutes, until cheese is melted and bubbly.

Sloppy Joes with Coleslaw

Ingredients for Sloppy Joes:

- 1 lb ground beef
- 1/2 cup ketchup
- 2 tablespoons mustard
- 1 tablespoon Worcestershire sauce
- 1 small onion, diced
- 4 hamburger buns

Ingredients for Coleslaw:

- 2 cups shredded cabbage
- 1/4 cup mayonnaise
- 1 tablespoon apple cider vinegar
- 1 teaspoon sugar
- Salt and pepper, to taste

Instructions:

1. Cook ground beef and onion in a skillet until browned. Drain fat. Add ketchup, mustard, and Worcestershire sauce. Simmer for 5 minutes.
2. For coleslaw, mix cabbage, mayonnaise, vinegar, sugar, salt, and pepper in a bowl.
3. Assemble Sloppy Joes by spooning beef mixture onto buns and topping with coleslaw.

Tuna Casserole

Ingredients:

- 12 oz cooked egg noodles
- 2 cans (5 oz each) tuna, drained
- 1 can (10 oz) cream of mushroom soup
- 1 cup frozen peas
- 1/2 cup milk
- 1 cup shredded cheddar cheese
- 1/2 cup breadcrumbs

Instructions:

1. Preheat oven to 375°F (190°C).
2. Combine noodles, tuna, soup, peas, milk, and half the cheese in a bowl. Transfer to a greased casserole dish.
3. Top with remaining cheese and breadcrumbs. Bake for 20-25 minutes, until golden and bubbly.

Black Bean Enchiladas

Ingredients:

- 2 cups black beans, cooked or canned (drained and rinsed)
- 1 cup shredded cheese (cheddar or Monterey Jack)
- 1 cup enchilada sauce
- 8 small tortillas
- Optional toppings: sour cream, chopped cilantro

Instructions:

1. Preheat oven to 375°F (190°C).
2. Fill tortillas with black beans and cheese, roll, and place seam-side down in a baking dish.
3. Pour enchilada sauce over the top and sprinkle with more cheese.
4. Bake for 20 minutes, until bubbly. Add toppings if desired.

Baked Mac and Cheese

Ingredients:

- 12 oz elbow macaroni, cooked
- 2 cups shredded cheddar cheese
- 1 cup grated Parmesan
- 3 cups milk
- 1/4 cup butter
- 1/4 cup all-purpose flour
- 1/2 cup breadcrumbs

Instructions:

1. Preheat oven to 375°F (190°C). Melt butter in a saucepan, stir in flour, and cook for 1 minute. Gradually add milk, stirring until thickened.
2. Add cheeses, stirring until melted. Mix sauce with cooked macaroni.
3. Transfer to a greased baking dish, top with breadcrumbs, and bake for 20-25 minutes.

Grilled Chicken Caesar Wraps

Ingredients:

- 2 cups cooked grilled chicken, sliced
- 1/2 cup Caesar dressing
- 4 tortillas
- 1 cup romaine lettuce, chopped
- 1/4 cup grated Parmesan cheese

Instructions:

1. Toss chicken with Caesar dressing in a bowl.
2. Layer tortillas with lettuce, chicken, and Parmesan.
3. Wrap tightly and serve immediately.

Ham and Cheese Stromboli

Ingredients:

- 1 sheet pizza dough
- 6 slices ham
- 6 slices Swiss or cheddar cheese
- 1 tablespoon mustard (optional)
- 1 egg, beaten

Instructions:

1. Preheat oven to 375°F (190°C). Roll out pizza dough into a rectangle.
2. Layer ham and cheese, leaving a small border. Brush edges with mustard if desired.
3. Roll up dough, tucking ends under. Brush with beaten egg.
4. Bake for 20-25 minutes, until golden. Slice and serve.

Pesto Pasta with Cherry Tomatoes

Ingredients:

- 12 oz pasta (fusilli or penne)
- 1/2 cup pesto
- 1 cup cherry tomatoes, halved
- Optional: grated Parmesan for topping

Instructions:

1. Cook pasta according to package directions. Drain and return to pot.
2. Toss pasta with pesto and cherry tomatoes. Serve warm or at room temperature.

Shrimp Tacos with Mango Salsa

Ingredients:

- 12 medium shrimp, peeled and deveined
- 1 tablespoon olive oil
- 1 teaspoon chili powder
- 4 small tortillas

Ingredients for Mango Salsa:

- 1 mango, diced
- 1/4 red onion, diced
- 1/4 cup cilantro, chopped
- Juice of 1 lime

Instructions:

1. Toss shrimp with olive oil and chili powder. Cook in a skillet for 2-3 minutes per side.
2. For salsa, mix mango, onion, cilantro, and lime juice in a bowl.
3. Assemble tacos with shrimp and mango salsa.

Veggie and Cheese Quiche

Ingredients:

- 1 pre-made pie crust
- 1 cup chopped vegetables (spinach, bell peppers, mushrooms)
- 4 eggs
- 1 cup milk
- 1 cup shredded cheese (cheddar, Swiss, or feta)
- Salt and pepper, to taste

Instructions:

1. Preheat oven to 375°F (190°C). Arrange pie crust in a pie dish.
2. In a bowl, whisk eggs, milk, salt, and pepper. Add vegetables and cheese.
3. Pour mixture into the crust. Bake for 35-40 minutes, until set.

Chicken Parmesan Sandwiches

Ingredients:

- 4 breaded chicken cutlets
- 1 cup marinara sauce
- 4 sandwich rolls
- 4 slices mozzarella cheese
- Optional: grated Parmesan for topping

Instructions:

1. Heat chicken cutlets and marinara sauce.
2. Place chicken on rolls, top with mozzarella, and broil for 1-2 minutes, until cheese is melted.
3. Serve warm, with optional Parmesan.

Steak and Potato Skillet

Ingredients:

- 1 lb steak, cut into bite-sized pieces
- 2 medium potatoes, diced
- 2 tablespoons olive oil
- 1 teaspoon garlic powder
- 1 teaspoon rosemary
- Salt and pepper, to taste

Instructions:

1. Heat olive oil in a skillet over medium heat. Add potatoes, season with garlic powder, rosemary, salt, and pepper, and cook until golden and tender.
2. Push potatoes to one side, add steak, and cook until desired doneness.
3. Toss steak and potatoes together and serve.

Lentil Soup with Crusty Bread

Ingredients for Soup:

- 1 cup dried lentils, rinsed
- 1 onion, diced
- 2 carrots, chopped
- 2 celery stalks, chopped
- 3 garlic cloves, minced
- 1 can (14.5 oz) diced tomatoes
- 6 cups vegetable broth
- 1 teaspoon cumin
- 1/2 teaspoon thyme
- Salt and pepper, to taste

Ingredients for Crusty Bread:

- 1 loaf crusty bread (store-bought or homemade)

Instructions:

1. In a large pot, sauté onion, carrots, celery, and garlic until softened, about 5-7 minutes.
2. Add lentils, tomatoes, broth, cumin, thyme, salt, and pepper. Bring to a boil.
3. Lower the heat, cover, and simmer for 30-40 minutes, or until lentils are tender.
4. Serve the soup with slices of crusty bread on the side.

BBQ Meatball Subs

Ingredients:

- 1 lb ground beef or turkey
- 1/2 cup breadcrumbs
- 1 egg
- 1/4 cup grated Parmesan cheese
- 1 teaspoon garlic powder
- 1 cup BBQ sauce
- 4 sub rolls
- 1 cup shredded mozzarella cheese

Instructions:

1. Preheat the oven to 375°F (190°C).
2. Mix ground beef, breadcrumbs, egg, Parmesan, garlic powder, salt, and pepper. Shape into meatballs and bake for 15-20 minutes.
3. Heat BBQ sauce in a pan and toss meatballs in the sauce.
4. Split the sub rolls, place meatballs in each roll, and top with mozzarella.
5. Broil for 2-3 minutes until cheese is melted.

Teriyaki Tofu Stir-Fry

Ingredients:

- 1 block firm tofu, pressed and cubed
- 1 tablespoon olive oil
- 1 red bell pepper, sliced
- 1 zucchini, sliced
- 1 carrot, julienned
- 2 tablespoons soy sauce
- 1 tablespoon honey or maple syrup
- 2 tablespoons rice vinegar
- 1 tablespoon sesame oil
- 1 tablespoon cornstarch (optional)

Instructions:

1. Heat olive oil in a skillet over medium heat. Add tofu cubes and cook until golden on all sides.
2. Add bell pepper, zucchini, and carrot, cooking for another 5-7 minutes.
3. In a small bowl, whisk together soy sauce, honey, rice vinegar, and sesame oil. Pour over tofu and veggies, stir to coat.
4. Optionally, whisk cornstarch with 2 tablespoons water to thicken the sauce and add it to the pan.
5. Serve over rice or noodles.

Veggie Burgers with Sweet Potato Fries

Ingredients for Veggie Burgers:

- 1 can (15 oz) black beans, drained and mashed
- 1/2 cup breadcrumbs
- 1/4 cup grated carrot
- 1/4 cup finely chopped onion
- 1 tablespoon soy sauce
- 1 teaspoon garlic powder
- Salt and pepper, to taste

Ingredients for Sweet Potato Fries:

- 2 large sweet potatoes, peeled and cut into fries
- 2 tablespoons olive oil
- 1 teaspoon paprika
- Salt, to taste

Instructions:

1. Preheat oven to 400°F (200°C). Toss sweet potato fries with olive oil, paprika, and salt, and bake for 20-25 minutes until crispy.
2. For veggie burgers, combine mashed beans, breadcrumbs, grated carrot, onion, soy sauce, garlic powder, salt, and pepper. Form into patties.
3. Cook patties in a skillet over medium heat for 4-5 minutes per side, until golden and crispy.
4. Serve the veggie burgers on buns with desired toppings alongside sweet potato fries.

Mini Personal Pizzas

Ingredients:

- 4 small pizza doughs (store-bought or homemade)
- 1/2 cup pizza sauce
- 1 cup shredded mozzarella cheese
- Toppings of choice (pepperoni, vegetables, olives, etc.)

Instructions:

1. Preheat oven to 400°F (200°C). Roll out the pizza doughs on a baking sheet.
2. Spread pizza sauce evenly over each dough.
3. Sprinkle mozzarella cheese on top and add desired toppings.
4. Bake for 10-12 minutes, until the crust is golden and cheese is bubbly.

Chicken Fajitas with Tortillas

Ingredients:

- 1 lb chicken breast, thinly sliced
- 1 red bell pepper, sliced
- 1 green bell pepper, sliced
- 1 onion, sliced
- 1 tablespoon olive oil
- 1 teaspoon chili powder
- 1 teaspoon cumin
- 1/2 teaspoon garlic powder
- Salt and pepper, to taste
- 8 small flour tortillas
- Optional toppings: sour cream, guacamole, shredded cheese, cilantro

Instructions:

1. Heat olive oil in a skillet over medium heat. Add chicken slices and cook until browned.
2. Add bell peppers and onion, and sauté until softened, about 5-7 minutes.
3. Season with chili powder, cumin, garlic powder, salt, and pepper.
4. Serve the chicken and vegetable mixture on tortillas with desired toppings.

Quick Shepherd's Pie

Ingredients:

- 1 lb ground beef or lamb
- 1 onion, diced
- 2 carrots, diced
- 1 cup frozen peas
- 1 cup beef broth
- 2 tablespoons tomato paste
- 2 cups mashed potatoes (prepared in advance)
- Salt and pepper, to taste

Instructions:

1. Preheat oven to 375°F (190°C).
2. In a skillet, cook ground meat and onion until browned. Add carrots, peas, beef broth, and tomato paste. Simmer for 5-7 minutes.
3. Transfer the meat mixture to a baking dish. Spread mashed potatoes on top and bake for 20 minutes, until the top is golden.

Spinach and Mushroom Lasagna

Ingredients:

- 9 lasagna noodles, cooked
- 2 cups ricotta cheese
- 2 cups shredded mozzarella cheese
- 1/2 cup grated Parmesan cheese
- 1 cup cooked spinach, squeezed dry
- 2 cups sliced mushrooms
- 1 jar marinara sauce

Instructions:

1. Preheat oven to 375°F (190°C).
2. Sauté mushrooms in a pan until softened.
3. In a baking dish, layer lasagna noodles, ricotta, spinach, mushrooms, marinara sauce, and mozzarella. Repeat layers and top with Parmesan.
4. Bake for 30-35 minutes, until bubbly.

Pork Chops with Mashed Potatoes

Ingredients for Pork Chops:

- 4 bone-in pork chops
- 1 tablespoon olive oil
- 1 teaspoon garlic powder
- 1 teaspoon paprika
- Salt and pepper, to taste

Ingredients for Mashed Potatoes:

- 4 large potatoes, peeled and diced
- 1/2 cup milk
- 4 tablespoons butter
- Salt and pepper, to taste

Instructions:

1. Preheat oven to 375°F (190°C). Season pork chops with garlic powder, paprika, salt, and pepper.
2. Heat olive oil in a skillet over medium-high heat and sear pork chops for 2-3 minutes per side.
3. Transfer pork chops to the oven and bake for 20-25 minutes, until cooked through.
4. For mashed potatoes, boil diced potatoes until tender, about 15 minutes. Mash with butter, milk, salt, and pepper.
5. Serve pork chops over mashed potatoes.

www.ingramcontent.com/pod-product-compliance
Lightning Source LLC
LaVergne TN
LVHW081332060526
838201LV00055B/2601